Precipice

Precipice

John Donoghue

John Donoghue [signature]

For Jim —
whose interest in this part
of me has always been a source
of support and encouragement — and
whose terrific grasp of English
has often bailed me out. I hope
you like these.

JD [signature]

FOUR WAY BOOKS
Marshfield

Cleveland, Ohio
April 3, 2000

Editorial Office
Four Way Books
P.O. Box 607
Marshfield, MA 02050
www.gypsyfish.com/fourway

Library of Congress
Catalog Card Number: 99-71363

ISBN 1-884800-28-9

Cover Painting, "Liquid Center," by David Haberman, by permission of the artist.

Book Design: Henry Israeli

This book is manufactured in the United States of America and printed on acid-free paper.

Four Way Books is a division of Friends of Writers, Inc., a Vermont-based not-for-profit organization. We are grateful for the assistance we receive from individual donors and private foundations.

ACKNOWLEDGMENTS

Agni: "Rabbits," "The Rooves of Toulouse"

The Cream City Review: "Stars"

The George Washington Review: "Efficiency"

Green Mountains Review: "Morning Walk," "Siren"

Marlboro Review: "The Well"

Oxford Magazine: "Rage"

Poets' League of Greater Cleveland Mirror of the Arts Performance:
"Concerto," "Old People"

Prairie Schooner: "Breath," "Hometown," "Reasoning With My Son,"
"Say Something Certain"

River City: "Blame," "Moraine"

Seattle Review: "Soup Bones," "Apologize"

The Virginia Quarterly Review: "Revision"

Willow Springs: "Eel," "Positive"

Wisconsin Review: "Geese"

For Carolyn—who was always there for the poetry—

and for Gabrial

CONTENTS

Prologue

III

IV

V

Prologue

REVISION

In Rwanda she gave her victims a choice: *Buy the bullet*
I will soon put through your head, or be hacked to death.
And here in this river, she doesn't raise that blue heron
from the shallows, she is the rising heron,
as she is the mother of napalm, destroyer
of the ozone, as she is my eyes that see this glass light
lapping at my feet: I've come to search the bottom
for things magical, and I have a pailful,

but I am sick to death of praising her, and sick
of her illusions—*language, consciousness.*
Look at me, she says, *and see yourself as*
separate and responsible: I'll *make your body,* you
drop the bomb—then act as if you came from someplace else.
See that desert's beauty?—I dried a sea for it.

I

ROOVES OF TOULOUSE

Not the blank wall to my left
despite its broad, pink face, almost all tongue,
fondling a contented *ahhhh*.
Nor the near wall, the same though smaller,
eyeless. And not the orange light from the ragged
tile roof, nor the roof's thousands of small,
self-important arcs, busily being roof. Nor the chimneys,
burdened as they are with their insolent antennas.

It is the tiny attic window that breaks
the roof's line like a whale's eye, pushing its filthy,
unused face into mine. The eye
never closes, though I left it
years ago; though I close it
and close it, in sleep.

BREATH

Memory's a flower the sky suffuses with light;
from here I can't tell if the flower is yellow
or white, if the sky's that evening purple
against the dense, black trees. And I don't know
why the man must be in his garden
on the slate path
through its center, beneath a tree.
Alone, he has left his meal to come out

and stand by the tree. It's the day I was born,
his only child, though standing there
he thinks there'll be more.
In fifteen years I'll threaten him
with a knife; tonight
he's relieved and happy.

STARS

Though it drives them mad—your terrible,
small face, born of their flaring disasters—
stay out there waving
your wind-bound flags. They can't cover
their ears, their eyes—they stare down, helpless,
from their great wheel of light, the moon
moaning, the zero of space
humming disapproval.

Glare at them—such weak lanterns—
what do they know of decisions and longing?
Raise the temperature: tell them
your theories of stars, show them
the photos. Can you hear
their hot teeth, grinding?

RAGE

Just five or six, he lies on his back in his dark bed
and what feels like tinfoil fills his mouth, the loosely
crumpled wad held carefully, its random corners
words he will learn; now,
just small points of pleasant
discomfort. So delicate a thing, he'll look back
surprised that it grew as he grew
to become the train wreck's twisted steel,

the collapsed remains of the burned-out building,
unyielding surfaces tearing his gums.
Moving his head so his fresh sheets
cool his cheek, he turns the uncrushed wad
slowly with his tongue, his mouth open,
controlled, and throbbing.

RABBITS

Last night's windless snow
built in the branches, and this morning's tracks
cross the back lawn
and lead down the small slope by the elm
to the woods. Why did I follow them fifty years ago
with a sling-shot and marbles? And why have killed
the jittery cardinals and thrushes?
What did I think death was?

The rabbit's great black eye
seemed always turned slightly away. I killed it
because I wanted to—wild, thrilling to uncover,
hard to kill. Afterward, I'd hold it by its feet,
blood still dripping from its nose, and throw it from me
into the woods—useless pelt, useless meat.

BURN

Let me burn. Do nothing. Let the room
fill with my mute smoke. Believe me, your concern
squeezes my tongue like a pliers, the red plum
plucked, its miserable heat
quenched in a bucket of someone else's
spit. *Don't* offer words—each one of yours
a split rivet
displacing one of mine—impoverished travelers

coughed from my throat. Here, take these matches
and light the whole pack; as the flame
sweeps and hisses
through the heads, hold them
to my neck. Only
my weakness screams.

SLAP

Eleven or twelve, I'm running on a street next to a friend
pedaling his bike. I've just hit an older boy with a stone
for calling me a name, and now as he chases us,
my friend yells that I won't get away,
that I must jump up
on the handle-bars. Afraid to jump, afraid I'll fall,
afraid we'll get caught, I keep on running.
Jump! he screams, until the older boy catches us both,

shoves my friend from his bike and me to the ground,
where he hits me over and over. Lying there in tears,
I have no way of knowing that of all of my childhood's
small defeats, this one will return again and again
to accuse me, and each time, at my friend's call,
I gladly reach for the bars and heave myself up.

DREAM

Outer surface smooth, like an egg's; logic
inward and complete; interior, a long,
twisting conversation—the charred
hand, the Nazis returned to Europe in their red and black
draped trucks, your call after the woman
who wordlessly hurried from your side.
Don't say anything. Don't examine the day's
residual anger. Instead,

pull on the polished boots, slip your arms into the uniform's
silk-lined sleeves, slip the red band onto your arm.
See?—your body has already rehearsed you.
Step into the street. Look—the woman has started to run.
For both of you it's so easy—one foot
in front of the other.

BLAME

It's possible to find a voice in the shore reeds
and in what the sky offers in flight: above the lake
yellow leaves stream down like a flock
to water. The black surface is life, not death, and the leaves falling
are memory: at the foot of a brown summer hill
a boy stands in the shallows, steps through the sucking mud
peering at reeds, examining the sky,
shouts from the float in the center coming easily

over the water. What could you have done, taunted
and beaten-up *out there?* O bright leaf,
bright boy, how I have hated us
for not killing one of them—not just any one of them,
the best of them—and for swelling me,
large tick, with shame.

II

MORNING WALK

Up ahead as one crow pecks at something in the gutter,
another calls out and lifts from the branch
of a sycamore. When you called last week to say they wouldn't
remove your lung—that you couldn't survive the severed
breastbone and broken ribs, couldn't take in enough
with what's left alive—I heard in your voice
all the hope you had for yourself
fall away.

It's the crows I look for now and not the large homes
that line the streets like postcards, each
with its trimmed lawn a brightly painted story
we have told ourselves
all our lives, and which the crows now untell
in their beautiful, flying voices.

GEESE

Swinging his thick arm to the place where geese
cross our broad, empty sky
he says, *Never kill geese.*
We are sitting on a stone wall, part of a small
stone church with a white steeple. He doesn't look
when I rest my hand on his knee. The sleeves
of his flannel shirt are rolled down
and buttoned. I think of him

wanting to be wise. *See how the geese*
belong to the marsh, he says, and as I look
shots bring three of them down. *Don't cry,*
he says; look how they fall like stones,
how broken they are, how easily they fit
in the dog's mouth.

OLD PEOPLE

Having it is bad, I'm not saying it isn't,
though the moment of being told you have it—
just before going in and then going in—
that's maybe worse: you hear it, and everything
falls to your feet like pots and pans.
We chew life and spit it out as it comes—even
that moment of being fingered,
though I wouldn't have believed it.

I cried once and I think smaller. Tomorrow
if they find more, I'm a goner. I knew someday
something would tap me on the shoulder.
It's like I'm on a train, I've passed
through a window—me on one side,
everything else on the other.

BLUE BUS

The woman across in the yellow house—Yvonne—
is as thin as a rail. Last year she drove her husband
each Tuesday to Monmouth General for radiation,
and I rode with them. Now who'll drive her?—
none of the bums around here, you can bet on that.
She'll have to take the blue bus.
They're very nice. Even when it snows they make
the village rounds, the only problem those raised

speed-bumps—each one they hit
there's so much pain. We don't talk much on the bus,
like yesterday when Evelyn, my friend
two streets over, got on. What can you do? You go
when they say, though some of us
barely make it to our stops.

WASHING

Around me has been another man who always spoke.
Helpless now to turn away, I stare down
at his rolls of fat, soap his sagging stomach,
stench of urine, I wash his groin.
Do this, he asked, and undressed easily
before me, for the first time.
He moans; he sucks air in
across his teeth from pain.

I want to do it. I want him clean.
I want this mouth of broken glass—
his drooping head, his red, raw cheeks,
my sorry conversation, sorry voice.
Who made this? Who made this even possible?
I did. I did.

WAKE

What have they done with his mouth? How *large*
it is. If you kiss him, if you lay your hand on his
hard hand—don't you see he's not dead, this just
the beginning? They in their parting woe, you in your sad,
pinched tie. He's yours—how much of him
can you feed, how much can you take home?
Start with his head—make it speak.
Heavy-lipped, thick-lidded, his head's too large

and he won't eat. He lives in a glass house,
hundreds of white-framed panes; he must
stoop, as he does now, turning from me, to enter.
The sky is an overcast gray—brighten it,
I cannot; a great, accreting mass
pulls at every word. I cannot make him speak.

SOUP BONES

He kneels on his father's grave and whispers
I forgive you. Headstones slam together, the earth
shakes its boxes of bones. *Ok-ok*, he says,
I forgive myself too. The sky darkens, the wind howls.
Ok! he yells into the dust—*I beg forgiveness!*
Ahh! smiles the mother-hen cemetery,
rearranges her bones, cluck-clucks her dead ones
back to sleep.

Defeated, the man mopes home—a rented room,
white ceramic bowl of soup, broad spoon.
I hate this place, he says. The table legs
beat the linoleum, neighbors
pound the wall, his soup slops his lap.
Ok! Ok!

MORAINE

The moraine is harsher in winter, its pocked slope
uncovered, its stones' white surfaces
pitched teeth erupting
in a disfigured mouth.
And this road I suppose its tongue,
and me, small thing,
passing unnoticed
from its lips. How tired I am

of my own easy wisdom.
The wave moves inexorably to the beach
and breaks. Frozen, it heaves itself
against itself, tearing the earth. And above,
the flat sun, obsessed with appearances,
hurries by in its jacket of white light.

THE GOODS

He's asking me why I've injured
my stomach, why my face is scarred.
He wants everything back: swollen feet,
arthritic elbow—I've lost some teeth, I joke,
hoping he'll look up.
A bare room, a desk, two chairs.
A suicide? he asks, I *don't like*
suicides. What's the difference? I laugh,

and then he does look up. His eyes
are slate-blue.
The *difference*, he begins—
but then a bell rings and rings,
and he writes *careless*
on his pad.

DANCER

He's not here today she coos to the drab,
library bindings, as if talking to children,
He's gone, James, isn't he? Robert?
Her gold earrings sparkle next to her long neck,
her blond hair's pulled back in a bun—
trim as a dancer she points to a small picture
cupped in her hand, says to the emptiness
at her side, *That's him, that's him,*

then catches me staring and stares back.
I bow my head, afraid
to look up. Oh dancer, before I begin the hum
of my own madness,
go away,
go away.

PRECIPICE

How many of these tall priests can line this street
before our course is altered? Their bright orange robes
already drive us faster than we want to go—don't you see
they're pushing us to that low wall and tree-line
ahead, where at this speed we'll slip turning
and fall to the river? With staffs
taller than they are—punctuation for their robes and bald,
brown heads—I'm certain they're leading us

into something, not away: stuttering,
that unguarded precipice, sour beds.
Listen—to—me!—the sidewalks are sliding—we must run
faster and stay, always, in the street.
Why can't they look away? Why are they banging their staffs
on the paving stones? Why are they moaning?

EEL

With its jaws clamped on my left calf, the thick eel
I caught one childhood Sunday from a bridge
has returned with me from a dream about food—
the wet knife laid flat on the cutting board,
floured pieces writhing in the pan.
Little snake, I murmur pleasantly (where is the sun
when you need it?) *you are just something I ate.*
Made whole again by dream, that great conjurer,

it bit down harder. *Listen*, it said, *despair's not the burlap
you held me with, not the black, threaded pipe
someone handed you. Despair sits in its room putting one
before two, its equations have no unknowns.* And that's
when I struck: *I was promised sea grass and mud*, it cried,
the body of a mammal. What is that rag? What is that knife?

III

REASONING WITH MY SON

His hand's locked hammer again
pounded the bough,
and this time, his first grip a fist,
broke it.
Then he tore two thick trunks
up from the mud,
their loud sucking a slobber
that made him grin.

And then—*whack! whack!*—
he beat the mud with them
until I left him there—splattered,
one trunk broken, his hands
whaling the other, unbreakable—
until dark.

SIREN

Getting up from my garden table that third time—
third loud siren
in less than an hour—and rushing to you inside
asleep on the floor,
I thought first that it's love, then
that it's fear that has me do it. Waking alone,
age four, and not find me,
panics you: *Why did you leave me!*

Why did you leave me! you screamed once
when I found you wild
with terror. *Do you think I would leave you?*
I'll never leave you,
my lie a nothing of words; my voice
what you wanted.

FEAR THE BODY

Not yet six and too independent, he gathers the few
fallen leaves I've missed and carries them to the front
before pedaling off out of sight. And if I too
wander out onto unlit ground, who can blame me for testing,
withdrawing from comfort and testing again
for the edge of that fear I follow, doggedly,
to its conclusion—it could have been him
decomposed in the ditch, it could have been us on the front page.

And if it was, and if our bodies sought comfort
from nature's murderous hand, their only mother,
who could blame them, poor stumbling beasts,
for finally nodding and yessing.
Look, we're already upstairs in his room, opening windows,
opening drawers.

GUIDANCE

On July 3, 1988 the USS Vincennes,
an Aegis missile cruiser stationed
in the Persian Gulf, mistakenly shot down
an Iranian airliner, killing all of its 290 passengers.

When spoken to he'd look away and mumble,
his face crimson, so I'd joke to unwind his knot, my own
not far from hand. Our brilliant senior—
when he couldn't find a job
I hired him. But the day he left for a weapons plant—
the only offer I'll ever get—he talked freely: *What if*
the systems I build kill thousands by mistake?
What if they shoot down the wrong plane?

No, no, I reassured him, *you'll discover*
your mistakes, and no one
has that much effect. Fifteen years
he has been there now. He had the brightest red hair
I have ever seen. He was the tallest, thinnest,
gentlest student. His hair was like fire.

POSITIVE

It's in his weak walk—his broad back and shoulders
held rigid, his drawn young face
pointed straight ahead.
Here on my small grass patch a bee
moves through the clover,
one flower at a time—the innocent
injury.　　　*How's it going?*
　　　　　O.K.

This morning's dawn was blue breath
blown like silk
across my back; now the day has swelled,
its red ear pulses and will not burst,
though fear jabs and jabs
with its long needle.

THE KITE

Above the narrow beach the gray sky blows cold
and the sand is cold. Help me fly this kite—
it's the rainbowed delta-wing that last year
lifted like a falcon from my hand; it now dives crazily
toward the sea. I've given it
all the slack I can. Please, with your young
exuberance, help me keep it
from the water. Yesterday I dove and struck a rock

just beneath the surface: my hands
hit first—fingers crumpled, palms bloodied—
no one saw me dive. Help me reel this in
so I can play it out again in bits
to break the dives. You never
could have dragged me in.

IV

WEED WHIP

Five of us in our five cars doing fifty
on this mountain road, close
through each dip and turn until this turn: the man
flashed through a break in the trees
and I've pulled over to watch.
Alone on the bare ridge, he swings the shaft
slowly back and forth. What could he be doing?
Heat presses through the window

at my face. What more will I learn
sitting here? The road ahead bends into trees;
later it will pass a rock face
drenched by a spring, then through a valley of farms.
And the four cars, close through the turns,
not far ahead, can still be caught.

INSIGHT

Professor Klein is lecturing in the great hall about boxes.
This is the top, he says, at once unsure where to point
since all sides look alike. *This is a corner,* he adds warily,
knowing up close that it's rounded.
This is the outside! he shouts into the dimness,
because I'm on the outside, and this
is what I see! There's an inside too,
certain now no one believes him.

Give me a knife and I'll prove it!
But on peering into the hall he discovers
it's empty—there's just this one box on the raised
platform, looking at itself,
trying to tear itself open from the outside in,
or the inside out.

APOLOGIZE

I take my memory to the dream street: twilight,
red-brick, two-story apartments. Less substantial
than mist, my self is sitting in a dark room—
I threw my food, I broke my plate.
I've come to offer you a way out, I say.
Please, little milliwatt, apologize. My self
doesn't answer. *Please, my American,*
my gigahertz, my seven-four-seven.

Outside, the street is dark, a few hydrants,
a dog—time to go and my self
won't budge. All right: How did I get here?
Where is the door?
Please, my sanity, says a voice,
pull up a chair.

CONCERTO

Plush seats, too much heat, and Itzhak Perlman
plays Mendelssohn. In the city today
copies of a man's genes were left at a sperm bank, the concerto
demanding, *Just how is it done?*, the orchestra—
all-knowing—refusing to stop, Mendelssohn shouting
Shut-up! I'm old! It's a detail!, the chorus of cough-drop
carrying ushers insisting, *The genes, the city's
technologies—all details!*,

so I stand and shout, *Hey, man! How—is—it—done?!*
The music stops and Perlman's pissed—
horrified, I beg forgiveness—*Just a thought!*—
the donor in the balcony applauds. Then Perlman
continues with Mendelssohn's genes—old music
we all somehow understand.

SPACE

Space knocks on my red door
answering the ad for the empty room: stooped, tired,
collapsed down to a point,
it talks of nothing but everything at once
in the same place. I argue for differences—
summer shade, ocean voyages—I stall for time,
space touching my face with hands
drained of heat. *No room!* I say,

space dragging me down
to the floor. *Once I was a seed,*
I sing, *once I filled nothing at all.*
Through the window—a black sky,
dense with stars,
where light moves freely.

FROM THE GLASS

The loud thump on the thick smoked glass
made me jerk up and look first at the gallery's window,
then, comprehending, for the bird. It lay
on the marble step and twitched; I didn't move to help—
who can save a bird? Across the small octagonal lawn
gardeners clipped an already perfect hedge, and a white fountain
played out unwavering jets. Crossing above,
that bird must have seen the other bird, identical to itself,

matching each of its last split-second moves.
Shaking for minutes, the bird at last stopped
and sat up—open-mouthed, dazed, one wing slack.
It will still die, I thought, even when its mouth closed
and it hopped to within an inch of the glass.
It seemed to stare in a long time, then flew off.

WALK/DON'T WALK

Black winter coat, rubber boots, green wool cap
pulled down to dark goggles—in the June heat
his approach a sudden summer storm.
Messages! he yelled, wanting to sell the dollar-sized
pieces of colored paper
pinned to his coat, his soaked body
extending its hand. *No, no,* I said, waving him off,
acting unafraid and nobody's fool. It was then

the box snapped and buzzed—
WALK! he shouted, *DON'T WALK!*
WALK! DON'T WALK!
JESUS! JESUS! JESUS!—the two of us
fearful, crossing together, one with messages,
shouting, one unable to buy.

BELLS

There is no explanation for the sound of bells
through my office wall, unless Gao next door
rings bells before he eats the home-cooked food
warmed each noon in the mailroom microwave.
Gao is certain to be sitting at a cleared table, his white dish
set in the center of the red kitchen towel
spread before him, certain now to be raising his head from prayer
and reaching with a movement empty of thought

for the small bell at the towel's edge:
    Mea culpa, mea culpa, mea maxima culpa—
Gao lifts the food to his mouth as bells
assemble again my abandoned priests, unshaven,
howling their loneliness past God
to a whitening moon.

MOONRISE

Darkness pours from the trees in waves like the pain
traveling my left forearm and shoulder. Towering clouds rise up
shaped like a face. I know I am responsible
for this pain, I know that the Earth is a gem set in a space
curved to hold it, and that the man next door
captures time and turns it
into light—*Just*, he says, *a point of view.*
Yet hard as *I* try, events still line up—one for pain,

one following with memory. Serious molecule, I stand and
stare across the yard to watch the moon slip free
and menace the night. *Speak to it*, I tell myself, *we're both bone*
fused in the same dying stars. Moon, I say, *I'm as blind*
and alone as you: everything we see—just light
at the surface of our eyes.

BEARS

Efficiency's small inner voice exhausts me,
counting and counting its minimums.
Offered the cut lawn in broad,
even stripes, offered the perfectly trimmed hedge,
it sees only the leaves'
future disorder, and it knows I keep bears
chained in the basement. *Don't go*, it pleads
when they shudder the load-bearing walls.

In winter's sealed house we huddle
by the glassed-in fire. *Promise me*, it asks
as it blankets my shoulders, and I promise.
Outside in its coarse web
strung above the street—from the turbines' bright steel
through the breakers—power hums in the lines.

FRANCE

I'm in the airport, and I'm *going alone to France!*
I'm going dream-like and alone to France
on Air France. But I forgot my clothes!
And I forgot my camera! And I get *lonely*
in a country alone. Yet I'm boarding the plane
going to France—first class, a movie,
alone. Now I realize I forgot my *passport!*
How did I get into this?! How did I not

think this through—going alone to France
without any clothes? Why *France?!*
Not France—some other big place. Well of course
I'm going alone to some other big place. Never mind,
I tell myself, life is like the movies—hop on a plane,
travel to France—*you just go.*

HOMETOWN

Her fingers would quiet me
when I couldn't speak or wasn't
about to speak. What did she suspect?
Blood was part of it; her voice
another part. There would be some pain,
then a quiet time, years maybe,
followed by change. Choose something
and live in its town, she said.

How long has it been?
I saw her once on the street and my questions
left me—that was long ago,
a different sky, different light. They say
she's back, young again, another family,
suffering smoothed from her face.

SAY SOMETHING CERTAIN

Recycle, recycle—the heart's bored. The sun tries
but fails to ignite the earth, its orange plumes
collapsing. And the poor earth
weeps for itself, its only moon a dull, cold place,
pulling and pulling its hair. Say something certain.
Take my unambiguous hand, this old spoon,
place a copper coin on your tongue
and say whole numbers. Say *Physics*.

Or if we've too much physics—make a wish.
Say you like the feel of my hair, my body
near yours. Outside in the hedge a tiny man with wings
rides a horse. Tell me death's precision is a dream
we'll wake from, like fruit gone good.
Promise me something.

HOOVES

Ill at ease on the mare's back,
the real horse
always more, the rider less,
he gallops her over a green field
and down the hillside,
her wide white flanks
stained yellow, her breath
heavy as they pass,

he grinning
and apart from her,
safely above
the shoeless hooves
that drum and cut the earth,
and are themselves cut.

SHE

Outside on the lawn a child sings its summer song,
light repetitions my body's strung steel
bleaches to whiteness. I cannot remember
my childhood: a boy composed years ago and written down,
he wanders in odd, stiff shoes.
Outside on the lawn the child stops as St. Ann's
rings the Angelus, black bells struck three, three, three.
I practice—I extend my tongue, its soft,

wet weight a dare, what enters my body stares out
through my eyes, swells my breasts—this is not
what I wanted—her body now sunk in mine. I will have
no womb. The shade slides in the wind, falls back,
the child begins to sing. How much can I leave,
how much recover?

OHIO

Ohio is again repairing our highway, one of two
south lanes torn up—I don't know
if I will get to you in time. They've dug through
the concrete base—large sections the men stand
waist-deep in; they've brought out their yellow machines,
put out their orange cones and barrels. To remember
your long fingers is easy, their ends flattened
as if hammered, the back of this wheel your spine's dog-leg

mid-way down, or the knots of bones in your shoulders.
Stopped, our line stretches to either horizon. I remember
how well you swam. Just ahead,
great swirls of white dust blow
toward the line, jack-hammers breaking up
slabs of stone. It's too much—I won't get to you in time.

TEACHER

I'm certain it wasn't me who put you
red-headed in my dream, stood you
before those sunlit windows
asking, *Why have you let me down*
after all you've learned?
What have I learned?
And why as I woke
did you turn to someone else?

And it isn't me who now burns you off—
mist from a river—your soft face, brilliant hair
standing in me with the certainty
of physics, stones
to worry in my mind's
agile hand.

RHODODENDRON

Let your feelings happen, you can't control them,
said last night's speaker at the Zen Temple, *Just go and do*
what you must do, so this morning I've hiked up
this tree-lined mountain road to find you—my embarrassing
dependent self with your thin, grasping arms.
The rhododendron are huge in bloom;
where the empty well-kept road winds down
either side of the ridge, I hold my own face

and kiss carefully my own lips. As the body's sweet terror
blooms and panics me, I can hear you—*The child*
does what it must do to survive—and feel you—a kind of
shadow marrow in a shadow femur, sending pain
through the body. Come out now, look up—
we have all grown old—they are gone.

PAPER

1.

The crying child gets up from his bed to look
for his father. He has dreamed of another family—
stucco farmhouse, dry weeds
blowing against a wall. In the dream, he enters the backdoor
and his dream father, sitting in the kitchen,
looks up and smiles. But now he's running through his real house,
confused by two fathers,
two places to live. In his parents' room he finds a comforting

mound of covers. *Dada!* he cries, just as a huge bear
sits up in the bed. Stunned, the child staggers and falls;
the bear snatches him up and runs from the house to the woods
behind the house, the child
hanging from its mouth, arms and legs
flopping, wide-eyed and dazed.

2.

Upstairs in the house his parents are talking
in bed—about what each would do
if the other died, recalling their own
real and longed-for parents. When their crying
son runs in the father sits up and smiles; the boy,
gaping, staggers and falls; his father
rushes from the bed and carries him back,
holding him to his chest.

And as if the body could save itself
by saying *real—dreamed,* by dividing
the sheet of paper into front
and back, so the father
holds his son to him and says,
Shh, it was just a dream.

THE WELL

The well descends as emptiness.
From its throat slips a heart,
mouth of blood,
heat brimming its stone lip. Who's singing,
    Blessed be the dumb,
     blessed be the stumbling mindless?
From the garden's far side
the boy's at once up from the bench,

his heart's fist running him
through the hedge's gap to his mother's
easy laughter on the lawn, to her own
fist in the earth.
Immovable, the well sings, its voice
brimming the air.

A native of New York City, John Donoghue has lived in
Cleveland, Ohio for the past twenty-seven years where he is
professor in the Electrical and Computer Engineering
Department at Cleveland State University. His poetry has
appeared in *The Virginia Quarterly Review, Prairie Schooner,
Willow Springs,* and elsewhere, and he holds an M.F.A. from
the Warren Wilson Program for Writers.

The Four Way Books Prize Selections in Poetry
1995-2001